About the A

Margaret Graham is the
twelve novels and has taught
many years. She is a member of the Society of Women Writers and Journalists, The Society of Authors, and The Romantic Novelists' Association (a previous Vice-President). She is Writer in Residence at Yeovil Arts Centre.

Margaret realised early on that her Stage 1 writing courses were doing more than laying the foundations of the craft. In fact, they were releasing a universal creativity that led her students towards many and varied areas of artistic and communicative endeavour.

In ***Writing Awake the Dreamweaver*** - in other words - writing awake the creative imagination, Margaret has distilled her years of experience into an accessible motivational handbook. It is one that will open the door to limitless creative opportunities.

Just as the aboriginals of Australia travel the Songlines, singing the ancestors' songs, singing the world into being anew, ***Writing Awake the Dreamweaver*** will help participators write into creative being, anew.

By the same author

Only the Wind is Free
A Measure of Peace
A Fragment of Time
The Future is Ours
Canopy of Silence
Annie's Promise
Look Within Your Heart
A Distant Dream
A Bitter Legacy
Out of the Night
Practising Wearing Purple
A Bed of Roses

Margaret Graham has written two plays, co-researched a television documentary, and written many short stories and features.

She has judged numerous writing competitions and taught creative writing for many years.

She is Writer in Residence at Yeovil Arts Centre.

Examples of praise for Margaret's books

Writing Awake the Dreamweaver

'The magic of Margaret. She's a force of nature. Inspirational.'
Rachel Cuperman, film producer and writer

Practising Wearing Purple

'First-class… a delightful novel, full of sympathy, understanding and drama…'
Tim Manderson, Publishing News

Only the Wind is Free

'Vivid, sensuous, warm-hearted, this novel marks a most impressive literary debut'
Barry Unsworth, Booker Prize winner

Canopy of Silence

'Superior and moving writing marks out this memorable story'
Daily Mail

Writing Awake the Dreamweaver

A motivational handbook designed to
release creativity

Margaret Graham

Margaret Graham

Audrey
I hope you enjoy!
Margaret

Wordforce Publications

First published in 2002 by Wordforce Publications,
East Court, Brook Street, Shipton Gorge,
Bridport, Dorset DT6 4NA
www.thewordforce.com

ISBN 0-9543724-0-9

A CIP catalogue record for this book is available from the British Library.

Printed and bound in the United Kingdom by
Creeds Printers, Broadoak, Bridport, Dorset

Wordforce Publications

For Vivien

With love and thanks for
all the years…

Acknowledgements

My thanks must go to the art and craft of writing. It has drawn out my creativity. It has given me my unique voice and shaped my communication skills. It has given me the confidence and insight to accept life's opportunities.

I would like to thank all my publishers, my agent, and, of course, my students for enhancing my life and my teaching. They have been, and are, a constant stimulation and example.

I met Kerry Cottingham in America. She's a graphic artist whose work I love. I feel privileged that she agreed to illustrate the jackets of my Dreamweaver series. Kate Pain has helped enormously with production. Thanks to her, too.

My gratitude goes, also, to my beloved family, and to the wonderful West Country in which I live. Also to my new discovery: the Cite de l'Ecrit, the literary quarter of Montmorillon, France. It was in this sublime medieval town, which is now my second base, that I felt inspired to embark on ***Writing Awake the Dreamweaver***, and the subsequent books in the Dreamweaver series. How could I not?

A definition of creative: having the ability to bring into existence, using **originality** of thought**, inventiveness**, **imagination**

'I need in a way to have a distinctive voice – a unique voice – to write in a way that no-one else does.'
Nikki Gemmell
Internationally and critically-acclaimed author

* * * * *

Release your creativity.
Reclaim your unique voice.
Reveal the communicator within.

Be the person you really are.

How?

By
Writing awake the Dreamweaver
A handbook designed to release creativity

It is a journey which will take a minimum of 6 weeks, and a maximum of however long you wish.

CONTENTS

Introduction

Releasing your creativity? Reclaiming your unique voice? Revealing the communicator within?

I can hear you asking, *'Idiot woman, my voice is who I am, isn't it? And, while we're at it, what's a Dreamweaver?'*

Your unique voice is who you were - a weaver of dreams.

Dreams born out of your distinctive creative imagination.

So, where is your imagination?

Once you were a child who wondered if maggots liked the taste of apples, and you weren't afraid to ask. Or a child who created worlds within clouds, or perhaps out of wallpaper patterns.

Maybe you stood in head-high meadow grass and urged ladybirds to rush home to their babies? Perhaps you listened to the distant trains and wove dreams into their passing? Or stared at factories and wondered at the thuds and thumps?

Maybe you talked to your friends and shared their fantasies, and explored ‘what if’ and ‘maybe one day’?

Or took the time to just ‘be’?

I bet you paid attention to the taste of tingling sherbet as you sucked it through a liquorice straw, and then laughed with sheer pleasure.

I’m pretty sure you reached out and touched the poppies in the fields and found them like - what? Tissue paper? Can you remember? Can you feel it now? Find some. Try it.

Did you close your eyes and see the red of the sun, feel its heat, smell the warm grass? Or maybe you heard the roar of the traffic and the clamour of a building site?

Once we were children who used all our senses to absorb life’s amazing textures, delights, and fears. We were children who created a world startling in its originality - a world unsullied by the perceptions of others.

We played soldiers, explorers, nurses, mothers, fathers and were really ‘there’, inside each of our characters, imaginatively creating their world, overcoming their problems, achieving their goals.

As we played, we grew in confidence, physically, mentally and emotionally, airing our thoughts with enthusiasm.

We were children who felt the fear of discovery, the heart pumping terror and pleasure of the chase.

We felt the thrill of challenge, the love for a baby doll, the taste of tea in the tiny, empty cups, the whoosh of tricycles, bikes, or roller skates.

We were children whose voices had not yet been conditioned by life and its rules.

We began to ask questions in our eagerness to explore this weird and wonderful world and its inhabitants, and were increasingly told, *'Not now, I'm busy.' 'Don't daydream.' 'It's none of your business.' 'Don't talk about Mrs Smith's warts again. It's not nice.' 'Just be polite, then people will like you.'*

We were children who were taught to fear, justifiably, and sensibly, and out of necessity. *'Look before you cross the road.' 'Don't go near the cliff edge.' 'Don't talk to strangers.'*

We were conditioned to 'fit in' to society's expectations.

And which of us would not do this for our own children. *'Stop playing that guitar and revise for your exams, because "chart" success is a pipe dream.' 'You want to act? Don't be daft, how will that pay the mortgage?' 'Writing, or painting, or music is not a proper job.'*

So, in time, we agreed. We ceased to express ourselves uniquely. Creativity became a dimly remembered distraction, an irrelevance.

Of course, this attitude was liable to change, if it could be considered an applied creativity.

'Applied creativity?'

This is something that has a socially acceptable result. It's useful, like painting the fence, making curtains, putting up shelves, cooking even. It gains the approval of others. It has a functional use.

Be aware that we deny or diminish our innate creativity at our peril. We need it.

It's how our heart sings, how our emotions and experiences can emerge into the light of the day and be accommodated and healed.

Our innate creativity supplies our unique voice, the one that views the world in its own inimitable way. It is what makes us what we are.

'Has my Dreamweaver gone forever?'

No, it's just in hiding, along with your self-confidence and creative self-esteem. In hiding and all but forgotten under the onslaught of the expectations of others.

So, how are we going to awaken, release, reclaim and reveal?

In Australia, the aboriginals sing their ancestors' songs whilst travelling along the songlines. (Bruce Chatwin writes movingly of this, in *The Songlines.*) The aboriginals sing the world into being, anew, and themselves into being as they do so. We're going to do something similar, but using the medium of writing.

We're going to write our creative selves into being, anew.

'But I don't know what to write about. I've never written. I haven't enough of interest to put down on paper.'

Once you focus in and begin to write, it's amazing how much you know, how much you have observed and remembered and tucked away in the recesses of your sub-conscious.

You're not going to be on your own. I'll be showing you the way and you can stop and recap at any time.

'How am I going to get started?'

I want you to try and give yourselves what'll seem the impossible, some time for yourself.

I want you to give yourselves an hour and 10 minutes a day for 6 weeks.

'Are you mad? That's out of the question. I have commitments, duties, I'm too tired after work. I can't do something that has no use, that has no accepted end product.' I can hear it now.

For a long time you have concentrated on those things that are 'correct'.

For a long time you have forgotten that other part of you, that crucial creative inner core. Without it you miss so much.

Think about it:

Would a request for private time from someone else be so impossible to grant?

So grant it to yourself.

Don't you have a right to the same consideration you give to others? Go on, try to find a good reason to turn away. It's not easy to come up with anything, is it?

But, on the other hand, if you can't manage all that time every day, then that's fine. Take that hour and 10 minutes and split it up over 6 days, 6 weeks, or months. In fact, whatever time scale you choose.

Writing awake the Dreamweaver is a creative journey and you apply your own rules. Set your own pace. Roads are for travelling along, not for just arriving.

Perhaps you're saying. *'All this sounds more trouble than it's worth.'*

It's not, I promise you. I want you to create with your unique voice. I want you to weave something glorious from your imagination.

I want you to learn how to play again.

I want you to relax, have fun and enjoy flexing your creative skills.

I want you to be sufficiently inspired to want to express yourself in writing for the purposes of this book, and then in whatever medium you feel is right for you.

I want you to communicate interestingly, and with ease for the rest of your life, absorbing, learning, receiving and giving.

I want you to realise that you can do all of this. I want you to be in control of your own development.

In this appointment with yourself:

We're going to begin the journey that'll help release the years of your life that you hold in your subconscious. In these years is the sum of your experience

We need to perceive with the heart of a child
and
the experience of an adult.

We're going to reach back beyond the 'you' that has become too busy with the rigmarole of life. We're going to summon back the child, that weaver of dreams. We're going to release your creativity, reclaim your unique voice and reveal the writer, communicator, artist, juggler or whatever it is that you are.

'Will it be a struggle?'

Probably, but also a joy.

'Will I be daunted?'

Probably, since we're often afraid of our own energy, and of unleashing our power and potential.

'Why?'

We fear it might change us, and affect the equilibrium of our lives, and so it might.

But consider this:

The equilibrium could actually be improved. OK, so we fear we might be considered selfish.

But consider this:

As we've said before, why should we deny ourselves private time, or the opportunity to develop and hone our skills, if we'd willingly give this time to someone else?

Progress might consist of two steps forward, and one back. That's how it often works, but let's go on, urged forward by the excitement of rediscovery. Soon horizons will expand, and abilities increase, perceptions will sharpen and enthusiasm smoulder until it explodes into life.

A few 'housekeeping' details before we proceed.

I have included a page for personal notes at the end of the sections in the book. Sometimes it's helpful to jot down thoughts, comments and ideas as you go along. I have also left wide margins for any notes you might care to make.

The designated time for the writing exercises are advisory only. You might find you need less, or more. That's fine. You're in control. You must do what's best for you.

Finally, if some of the exercises take you to traumatic areas, places you'd rather not go, stop. Stop and ditch the book, or hand it on to someone else, or pick and choose the exercises, or adapt some to suit yourself, or create quite different ones.

Get used to taking control, to saying no, to looking for alternative ways of proceeding. I am only here as a guide, not as a rule maker.

Personal notes

Section One

Now, let's work our way through the hour and ten minutes.

The first 20 minutes

At some stage of the day, to suit yourself, I'd like you to do what I find essential for my work as a creative being. I write stream of consciousness for 20 minutes. This helps unlock the door to immense creative possibilities.

'Stream of consciousness, what's the woman whittering on about?'

Stream of consciousness is simple, just a stream of thought pouring out onto the page. In its finest form, edited and crafted, it can be seen in work by authors such as Virginia Woolf or James Joyce. You don't know them? Read their books. Try to find a biography. Curiosity is our ally. It leads us on.

'So this stream of consciousness..?'

We're going to use stream of consciousness every morning. We'll start to access our creativity by letting our thoughts run out of our head, down our arm and through into the pen or pencil onto the page, unedited and without shape.

We'll let it all pour out of us. I say 'we', because I'll be doing it too. It's part of my life now.

We're going to write for 20 minutes.

'Did you say pen or pencil?'

Yes. Discard the keyboard for this exercise.

'Why?'

Because something happens when we have a pen or pencil in our hand. The pen becomes joined to the creative imagination. It also means that we can write anywhere, any time. In a tent, a hotel room, a railway station. No excuses.

Try. It's not difficult, I promise.

I write the daily pages when I am alone. I let my thoughts run as they will.

Amongst them will be problems. They might be problems that I didn't know were pushing at me, longing to be addressed.

Or I might write down a dream I might have had that night. I write my hopes and fears. Never forget the fears. We all have them. Too many.

But most of us embark on opportunities anyway.

I watch the words take shape. I know that they're better out than in. I pour out my joys, my reservations, my observations.

Each day, I write down something - even it's only that I'm bored, angry, confused, happy, tired, sorry for myself. I ask, or tell myself, why I'm feeling these things. If I don't know then I will write down that I don't know.

Or I might consider changing my shampoo. Would another make my hair seem thicker? Or I might write that I wish that dog wouldn't bark. I write about big and little things.

'Must it be 20 minutes?'

If at all possible, but ultimately it's up to you. You must remember that you are in control. I'm merely guiding you, as my early creative writing teachers guided me. Write in some shape or form, though. I think you'll find that it'll make you feel better. I find it empowers me to see my very own thoughts and opinions. They have a right to be there, in black and white; the trivial and the important.

The daily pages oil the wheels of imagination, they flush out half-remembered experiences and observations. They drive us on. We'll think, I didn't know I knew that, felt that, remembered that. They'll stretch us. Try and write the pages every day for the rest of your life but, if not, then for the duration of this journey we are taking together.

If the morning isn't right for you, then choose your own time.

But, maybe it would help if I gave you a few tips to help prime the flow until you truly catch the habit?

For instance, if my mind is a blank and I'm writing with a pencil, I'll ask myself how it feels. Is it pressing into my finger? Is the lead dark, or light? I'll let my mind wander out of my head, down my arm, into my hand.

I write. I'll ask myself questions. Perhaps the chair creaks. Why? Do I find it annoying? What else annoys me?

Try the ticking of the central heating boiler. Is it regular? Where have I heard that before, or something similar? Perhaps it was an uncle who irritated me. Why? His jaw clicked when he ate. Some might say, how arrogant of me to be irritated. Maybe it is. These are my thoughts, my memories. I need honesty from myself if I'm to find my creative core, if I'm to connect to other people and their thoughts and feelings.

Perhaps my uncle's clicking jaw annoyed him as well? How awful. He was stuck with it whereas I could move away. And so on, and so on.

Still not working for you? It's not a problem. Can you hear the rumbling of the traffic? Write it. Where are those people heading in their vehicles? Who are they? Is someone back seat driving? Is someone else a road hog? Why? How else does this aggression manifest itself?

Instead of a pencil, are you using a pen, or ballpoint? How does that write? At what angle do you hold the pen? Can you smell the ink?

Are you at a table? Is it smooth? Is it wooden? Is there a grain? How does that grain feel if you trace it with your finger? Observe it, feel it. Write it.

It's the little things in life we remember. There's the school desk, with carved names, or the smell of chalk. It's similar details in everyone's past that hold us all together. Use these to connect to others in your work.

Write down any stray thoughts that are trying to nudge their way to the fore.

Welcome them, for from them will come others bearing truth, perhaps long forgotten.

Remember not to worry about those little irritants called full stops, capital letters and commas. Toss them aside if they don't come naturally.

Remember not to fret about spelling. Ignore anything that tries to inhibit or control your thoughts. We're trying to break the barriers of conditioning, we're after the unique, real, unvarnished you.

Remember all the time that every word you write is yours. It owes nothing to anybody else. You're the one holding the pen.

Let the thoughts run free - the good, the bad and the ugly.

Forget rules. Forget that you were told never to say anything bad about anyone. Forget that you're too busy, really, to do this.

Write down anything, everything. Remember that if you ask a question and don't know the answer, say so.

This isn't a test. Ask yourself why you don't know. Let one thing lead to another.

Write down praise for yourself. Have you done something good for someone else? Do you feel pleased? Say so.

Have you had some success? Say so. Success is sweet and should be savoured.

Are you tired? Say so. Why are you tired? Try and avoid that situation from now on, or pace yourself differently. You don't have to exhaust yourself to have validity, you know.

You might find that your words and thoughts transcend your experience. Welcome to the 'creativity club'. The club where you say, *'Now, just where did that little gem of profundity come from?'*

These gems come from that instinctive and uninhibited source deep inside, and all around everyone. Welcome them.

See these gems as the stirring of the Dreamweaver, that lost and forgotten child peering through the gates from the depth of your life.

This is the child, this 'you' of days gone by, who'll unlock your creativity.

Let the stream seep, bubble, flow. Keep going.

Go on, no-one's watching, listening, reading over your shoulder. Go on, in 20 minutes I can manage two pages. If I don't feel like doing two, then I do one. Or perhaps gallop to three.

Don't read back. Don't seek perfection.

Perfectionists hide behind the next rework, and the next. They want to stall. They're too tentative to explore, too frightened to step that one foot beyond the boundaries of the familiar. They seldom finish. At this stage we don't want any re-writes, any editing. That will come later when you pursue your chosen path.

You're not a staller. You're going to plonk on that pith helmet, slip slap the mosquito repellent, and stride out into the jungle, searching for 'you'.

Incidentally, if you come across words you don't understand, either in this book or somewhere else, take a moment to check them in a dictionary. I do it all the time.

Now, back to the business in hand. When you've finished, destroy the work.

'What – you cannot be serious?'

I thought that would ruffle a few feathers. I am absolutely serious.

You're unlocking your mind, honing the channel. The stream of consciousness will carry debris. Debris can be profound, trivial, superb, ugly, resentful, angry, painful, anguished, unfair, biased, savage, especially if you're writing post-spouse-row, post-demotion-angst, post-shameful-thing-I-did yesterday, post-whatever-is-bugging-you-right-now.

Above all, it'll be private.

Destroy the pages.

You've said it. You've allowed your mind to range beyond conventional politeness, beyond conditioning, beyond kindness, beyond social expectation.

You've attacked, you've confessed, you've asked questions, you've laughed, you've written of a stunning sunset, or of a lover you once knew, of your pride in yourself.

Destroy the pages or you will be inhibited in what you write. You will fear that others might find it, and read it.

All through your life there will be debris to sort.
Write. Exorcise. Understand.

It'll lead to tolerance, of yourself and others. It'll lead to empowerment, to the strength to say NO, and the courage to say YES.

Trust that if you leap,
you'll be taught to fly.

Sometimes I add a statement at the end of my daily pages. If I'm feeling a bit fragile and put upon it could be, *'I'm worthy of respect.' 'It's important to find out who I am.' 'Come on, I can do this.'*

OK, maybe it sounds a bit corny, but an American tutor suggested it years ago. It can be helpful, or just irritating. That's up to you to decide. I veer between the two.

Personal notes

Section Two

Let's pencil in an appointment for another 20 minutes with yourself, every day, or as your pattern dictates. We have that hour and ten minutes to use up, remember.

The second 20 minutes

Just be alone again, for 20 minutes. Indulge me in this.

'What am I to do now?'

Simple, do something you want to do.

Twenty minutes on your own to do something you want. Is pleasure so hard? Does it always have to be justified, earned? I think not.

What will you do? Whatever it is, I'm asking you to pay attention while you do it. We need to get used to just being in the moment. We need to become childish again and look no further than the now. You owe it to the child you once were, and the creative person you are helping yourself to become.

I think this is what used to be called daydreaming, just 'being', paying attention to the now and letting your mind wander along its own path. When we were children they used to say, '*Stop daydreaming and listen to me.'* Do you remember? Now you must start daydreaming, please.

Maybe you'll listen to music. What instruments are playing? Can you hear each one, or not? Let your mind poke and pry, let your senses listen, feel, see, smell, taste, remember. Let your mind follow the memory or the image.

Rather than listen, you might want to play your own music. Perhaps you'll play the drums to a Rolling Stones CD?

You've no drums? What about a pan and wooden spoon? Was this your drum kit when you were young?

Can you remember the feel of the spoon on the pan, the vibration up your arm? No? Then do it. Did you rest it on your knee? Did the edges of the pan cut in? Try now and see.

Or will you dance? If so, in tap shoes, or barefoot? When did you last dance barefoot? When did you last want to dance, but didn't? Why? What's the best dance you have ever been to? What is the worst?

My worst was as a teenager, a 'Ladies Excuse Me'. That dates me. I asked a gorgeous Italian who had sat out every dance at a Young Farmers' hop. He stood and was no taller than when he was sitting. He spoke no English.

My friends laughed all through the dance. I was angry with the gorgeous Italian for being so short, and with myself for minding. I was angry with them for laughing and with myself for wanting to laugh, because it was funny in a black way. And then I felt ashamed.

Oh, such a gamut of emotions, such memories. One day I might even remember the music. It's the only blank. If I can't, I'll have to accept the fact. I remember the emotions though. I can feel them. I could write them. I've written them in another context. That's what writers do. They use their experiences to log into the feelings of their readers, via their fictional characters. Writers discover they can empathise and that it's crucial to their work. It's crucial to whatever creative endeavour we undertake, and to our relationships with others. We need to reach deep inside ourselves to stimulate our creative imagination, in order to communicate at all levels.

If you simply, absolutely, can't do something specifically for yourself on a given day, make it your moment anyway. While you prepare vegetables for a meal, pay attention to the rhythm, the breathing, the chopping.

Is music playing on the radio? Is there silence? Is there ever really silence? When did you last 'hear' silence? When did you last long for silence?

Does the aroma of the food you are preparing feed your mind with images? Does it help you revisit the years held in your mind?

If you're ironing, is the iron heavy? Did your mother have a steam iron? Where did she iron? When was the first time you ironed?

Did you ever love someone so much that even ironing their clothes was a intimate pleasure? Is it still? If not, why does the feeling fade, become something else? Does it become stronger, or weaker?

Ask questions of yourself and situations. It stirs the Dreamweaver.

Do you have children? What are they doing? How are they doing it? How can you tell whether they are happy, sad, thoughtful, attentive, dreaming? Do their moods trigger a half-forgotten childhood memory?

Are you in an office, on the shop floor, at lunch with your mates, driving a van? When you next park, listen, look, please pay attention to the way the door of your van opens. Does it squeak? Which muscles are you using? Notice the movement of the van as you leave.

Do you make your children's sandwiches for school, or your own? Do you follow the pattern set by your mother or father? What were the fillings way back?

When did you first make your own sandwiches? Did you make the sandwiches for your siblings?

Were you the sensible one?

Did your 'label' create an expectation that has been difficult to alter, to escape? How has it dictated your life? How has it denied you opportunities?

When you were a child, could you have been different if you were the youngest, instead of the oldest? What would it have been like if you had been the youngest?

What does it mean to be the youngest, the oldest, the middle? The only? Think about it, imagine. If you can't imagine, ask someone who has experience of that position within the family.

Who knows, you might set them on the path to creativity.

On the other hand, your childhood situation might have been more complicated. Write about that, if you wish.

Please note that from the 'paying attention' will come the opening, questioning mind, the understanding of yourself and others, the opening up of your creative world, the ability to ask questions which raise the interest of the person approached.

You will ask questions, and improve your ability to listen and raise your communicative confidence. You will cease to fear appearing foolish.

At the end of the 20 minutes, write it down if you want to. Go on, be greedy, give yourself some extra time. But make it an extra. Do not dip into the last 30-minute slice of 'our' hour. We need that.

'But why are we doing all this?'

It's to get into the habit of giving ourselves permission to have the time to be creative beings.

'*But...*'

It's to help you understand the world about you. It's to help you empathise. To help you sympathetically imagine. To help you bring your work alive, to make it believable, and enhance your own world.

If we're to be writers, we need to be able to beckon our readers into the world we have created. Our readers need to sit in our character's chair, and feel the texture of the cushion.

We need to reach out and touch our reader in long-forgotten places.

We need to connect with their past, present, and future: their Dreamweaver.

If we're to be artists, we need to bring this to our canvas, potter's wheel, or whatever medium is our chosen one. If we're to be readers, we need to appreciate this within the prose. If we're jugglers or trapeze artists, or any sort of creative being, it will help give us the confidence to dare to miss, to fail, in order to reach the heights. It will help us work out what will enthral our audiences, what will raise the tension, what will keep them with us.

Remember why you're doing this when someone asks, in the absence of any visible end product, *'Why are you wasting your time?'*

You're writing, and you're on the journey of a lifetime. You're tracking down that unique voice of yours. You're on a journey and there's merit in the journey alone.

Are you still doubtful about your justification?

Just think to yourself that the days will pass whether or not you're spending time in this way.

Each day another day older, so why not be wiser, why not explore, why not take firm steps into the empowering landscape of the creative world?

I want you to be the best that you can be. I want you to be creatively inspired. From the moment you begin to write awake the Dreamweaver, you'll see differently. The world will be endlessly fascinating. Every new day will have something to offer.

Try and find time to read every day to help your mind absorb and understand the concept of form, organisation and communication. If you don't have time to read, watch drama. Soaps are fine.

Personal notes

Section Three

For the final slice of the hour, I'm asking you to complete a series of writing exercises. A bonus here: this writing you keep.

The last 30 minutes

These exercises have value in themselves, but might also be the germ of an idea. An idea which might shape up into a short story, a novel or a poem, a painting, a piece of pottery, a song, a talking point.

Use these exercises to probe, to think, to ask questions of yourself, or others. If these questions are unanswerable, or you can't quite remember, what do you do? Use your Dreamweaver to imagine

I suggest you read through the exercise in the morning, and let your mind mull it over throughout the day. By the time you reach a convenient writing time, I think you'll be raring to go.

A regular time is best, but not essential. For instance, I wrote my first few novels snatching at time whilst my children played around me - phew. It was fine, as long as I had created enough thinking and dreaming time during the day.

First set of exercises

Day 1

Write about your childhood bedroom. For 30 minutes. That's all. Not just a description, but be in it. What can you see outside? What can you hear going on in the rest of the house? Do you like your bedroom? Do you have to share? What about the dreaded bunk beds? Are you top or bottom? Do you like what's going on in the rest of the house? Be there in the daylight, and in the night. How are the sounds different?

Write for 30 minutes.

Write for longer if the spirit moves you, and you dare to give yourself the wicked gift of time. Go on, go for it.

Day 2

Write about a childhood friend. Be there, back in the past, together, or in the gang. What are you doing? What does your friend's voice sound like? How does he/she move? Why is he/she your friend? What aspect of you has brought about this relationship? Where is he/she now? You don't know? Then imagine. How do your feel about him/her now? What did you feel back then? If you haven't kept in touch, do you wish you had?

Day 3

Write about a child you disliked. Be there. I remember a member of 'our' gang. She had a snotty nose. Would I have liked her if she hadn't? Who knows? Was she embarrassed because of her nose? Did I approach her differently because she had that nose? Did I alienate her? Is this why she was correspondingly nasty to me? And for goodness sake, why didn't her mother tell her to have a good blow? Should I have told her? Didn't I care enough? Wasn't I brave enough? Did I consider it wasn't my problem? Or that it wasn't polite? Should I have minded that snotty nose?

Was I judgmental and arrogant? Probably, but why do these things put us off, quite as much as they do? Why on earth don't we look somewhere else? Somehow we can't.

Don't shy away from exposing yourself as arrogant or judgmental. It's not pleasant to strip the veneer of 'sweetness' but it's important if we're to track down who we really are, if we're to find that unique voice.

So, what can I remember beyond that nose? Pale eyes. She was big, bigger than the rest of us. And her hair? No, I can't remember. But now I can see the way she moved - slowly and carefully.

So, in all honesty, did I feel guilty about my behaviour at the time? Do I in retrospect? Do I regret my attitude from a position of maturity? Well, yes, actually, but at least now I am in a position to understand, and to write from the point of view of children of that age. Just as we all are, if we can work our way back to that existence.

One day, we were all sitting on the kerb in the avenue and our teacher walked by. It caused a great ripple. Our mothers were furious that we'd let them down. *'Sitting on the kerb, indeed. Inside at once.'*

That tells us a lot about how much appearances mattered back then. Was it just a facet of society then, or more particularly one's own circle, even one's own family? Does it still exist?

Think about it. Try and understand every memory you unearth. OK, so I have diverged. That's good. When awakening the Dreamweaver that's good. It's only much later that those destined to be writers need to consider relevance, form and shape.

We'll discuss that further in *The Writer's Springboard*, the next book in the Dreamweaver series, but don't forget that there are many other books published on the basic techniques of writing as well.

Day 4

Write about your favourite game or toy, for 30 minutes, but using your own handwriting. There's more though. Use the hand you would not normally write with.

I want you to have to think consciously about the act, just as you would have done when you were learning to write as a child. I want you to understand the explorations and hurdles of childhood.

So which game or toy was your favourite? Mine was a hobby-horse, made out of a broom handle and Dad's stuffed sock which could be darned no more. That's interesting. People don't darn anymore. I can see the green wooden darning mushroom my mum would place in the sock, as she sat listening to the radio in the evening. I'd forgotten that. It's an image that sums up a period: post-war, pre-television, the years of make and mend.

Allow yourself to follow the stray memories. If something niggles you, and you want to know exactly when television came in, and when it stopped closing down at a child's bedtime, then go and research. A scary word, but it's simple, and leads to good moments.

Try the library. You'll find your local librarians are wonderfully helpful. Sue Bramble at my local library in Martock, Somerset, was superb, though now I've moved I find the ones in Bridport and Burton Bradstock equally good.

Or there's always the Net, the museums, the horse's mouth. In other words, people who have experienced such times.

Back now to the toy which heralded endless games. I wasn't riding a hobby-horse around Dad's veggie patch, but a stallion across the plains. Sometimes just riding, at others on a mission, overcoming obstacles. If I was with friends, some would be goodies, some baddies, but always there would be a leader. Always the 'mission' scenario was exciting, and reaching our goal was satisfying.

The other game, that of just riding, was an interlude, a pleasant way to pass the time. Once you've remembered your childhood toy, think of a time when you constructed a game, and achieved a goal.

In other games, I might have been a nurse, or sometimes I'd have to take the boy's role. Did you play games in which there was a gender change?

Make sure that you observe both sexes as you go about your days, because by now you'll be observing, and eavesdropping. Don't be too obvious, for down that road leads slapped faces.

'It's my job,' you say firmly when your spouse, or friend objects. One of the great joys of these exercises is the requirement to be nosey.

You see, I want you to be inside the skin of others. It not only leads to a certain tolerance, but helps you to express the emotions and personalities of others.

Day 5

Write about autumn when you were a child. Isn't it just fantastic? Do you remember the sight of the leaves, the ploughed fields, the sound of it; the crackling leaves and bonfires? What about the scent of fallen apples, wood smoke, and the taste; those baked spuds in the bonfires, and hot porridge in the morning? How about the feel of conkers as they twang on their strings, and the wind as it dries your lips?

Why do leaves change colour? Would it be an idea to find out?

Curiosity is essential in a creative being.

As children, my sisters and I would be encouraged to rake up leaves, and were then fed crumpets by the sitting room fire. The butter oozed...

Did the fire glint? I can't quite remember. I'll say it did, but on what? Perhaps the fire-irons? Yes, I remember that, or think I do. I remember the butter on the plate, and a few crumbs, and wishing there was more. I remember my mother saying it was better to feel like that. It kept the taste alive.

Actually I'm not sure she did say that, but it just came into my head, so I'll keep it. It sounds like her. It looks good on the page. My creative self is at work.

One year, we roasted chestnuts on a shovel. The shells were blackened more one side than the other. What did we do with those shells? Was Dad there? What else was going on in our lives at the time? Go on, think hard about yourself.

At this stage, I must mention that a student of mine took me to task because she was a city child, and autumn meant nothing to her. There were no trees where she lived, and swirling leaves. But she remembered the summer; the street play, the shadow of the walls on the cracked pavement, the heat beating upwards. So write about summer, I said.

Remember. Write from your own experience, adapt the exercises. You're in control. Nothing's set in stone. Don't be afraid to challenge anything.

Day 6

Time out.

On the sixth day you will disregard the 30-minute slot. Instead, you'll take as long as you like to give yourselves a treat. You'll walk on the beach, shop, whatever. Alone or with someone.

Treat time is important. It keeps the stress of life under control. When I was very busy, I forgot to allow myself that time. It was a mistake. Take it, you'll work better for it.

Treat time recharges your batteries, and allows your mind to lie fallow, and inspiration to enter.

Personal notes

The next six days

By now you've had your day off. But did you stop looking, listening, thinking? I doubt it. You're digging and delving, you see. You're writing yourselves into being, anew.

We must be firm and give ourselves the hardship (!) of listening to the conversation at the next table, or on the bus.

We must think, remember, pay attention, be curious, provide answers - it doesn't matter whether they're true. Remember you're a creative being, a weaver of dreams. You're releasing, reclaiming, revealing.

This week, you might feel tired, nervous, off balance. You might feel a bit edgy, vulnerable. Keep on, it's happened to us all. You're stirring up the years, you're becoming 'aware.'

You might be wondering if it's worth all the hassle.

You might be working up that *'Oh do I have to?'* feeling. That *'Do I have to walk the dog? It's raining.'* That *'Do I have to do Margaret's daily pages? Let her do what she wants with her stream of consciousness. I've nothing to say. It's tedious. Boring.'*

You'll be fine once you get going. No excuses. Some days you'll think there's nothing there, waiting to rush from your mind, onto the paper. But try the triggers I suggested earlier. Let me remind you.

The first slice

The daily pages.

Listen. What can you hear, see, smell, touch, taste? Maybe the ticking clock, the light falling on the table, the feel of the pen, the taste of toast? Is that really nothing? See where it leads, but if it's to nowhere, then that's fine. Just try something else.

This is what creative beings do. They can't lie on a chaise longue eating peeled grapes, and waiting for inspiration. They work. They keep going.

Conversations, or 'work in progress' have small beginnings. There's a reaching out in trivia.

Write. Do these pages. You'll produce psychological truths. You'll exercise your creative mind.

When it starts to flow, be fascinated by the debris. Look at it from this angle, from that angle. The past is us. Learn of it, from it. Soon you'll use it, manipulate it to serve the 'present' you. By doing so, you'll exorcise ghosts, make them manageable, spring clean that emotion which has subconsciously been driving or draining you.

Relax, allow the past the right to exist, to inform our work, as well as our lives.

You'll find joy amongst the memories, you'll remember old friends, good times. Savour, roll it all around in your head.

There'll probably be guilt. So what's so special about you that you are not entitled to a mistake, or a trillion of them. Are mistakes just for the rest of us? Is guilt the preserve of everyone but you? Come on. How else do we learn?

OK, some of it brings pain. Face it and step beyond your comfort zone to learn from it. But, I repeat, if you really don't want to go to some dark places, just say NO and stop.

Write out of the heart of a child
and the experience of an adult.

Personal notes

The second slice.

Remember to allow 20 minutes for your time alone later in the day. Do something daft. Try finger painting. How long does the paint take to dry? Does the smell of the paint take you back? What colours have you chosen? Pick up a brush. No art brush? Then try a decorating brush. No paint? What about emulsion?

Paint what you feel. No specific shapes, just splodges, or a curve if that's what you want. With this one daft moment you've added something to your bank of experience, you might have nudged a childhood memory.

You're one step further on. Think how you've progressed in just six days. There are words written that hadn't been considered last week, thoughts thought, questions asked and perhaps answered.

Remember not to judge yourself too harshly. Praise yourself instead, for work you've done, time you've spent.

Remember to play, to take that time out every sixth day, without fail. From now on, I'll try not to nag you over the daily pages, or the time alone. You'll do the best you can to find the time, and if you can't, so be it.

Just remember that this is not an exercise in stress. It's to be enjoyed. Work at your own pace. Alter the exercises to suit yourself. Use them in the future if you need to.

'Why would I want to do that?'

At some stage, you might feel a block in your creativity. Pick out an exercise with a pin. Do it again. Compare it with the first time. Have you remembered more? Have you seen things differently?

Personal notes

Second set of exercises

Day 1

Read the opening pages of Laurie Lee's *Cider with Rosie*, and see the grass, smell it, hear the sounds.

Look back at the exercise where you wrote with the wrong hand. You imagined then, what it was like for you all those years ago. Now see things from the height of that child.

Come on, down you get. Let's make you into that small child, or slightly older, or younger. It's up to you.

Now, be yourself at that young age in Woolworths, or some other department store. Do you remember all those counters you couldn't see over? Remember losing your mother? All you can see are legs.

If you weren't lost in a store, where were you lost? Feel the fear.

If you were never lost - imagine.

But before you concentrate on this exercise, it might help to read on for a moment.

Fear.

We're all familiar with it. It dominates our lives if we let it. It can inhibit us. It can rule us. Think about it. Face it. As children we were taught to fear. It kept us safe.

Fear, though, can cause us to avoid opportunities.

Perhaps we fear failure or humiliation? We fear the dark, or what might happen if..? We're frightened of not living up to the expectations of others, of not being 'nice' enough, of letting others down. We fear love, rejection, commitment, disapproval. We fear that old unmentionable – death.

The revelation - that we are not mortal - seems to take forever to come to come to terms with, if we ever do.

Do you remember that moment of discovery as a child? The knowledge took the glow of safety from our lives. We tend to think we are alone in coping with this huge discovery but we're not.

Most people have hit this wall, tucked it away, and let the fear wriggle about. I can't remember how old I was, but not very. I used to lie in bed with my hand on my heart, just checking it was still ticking.

I used to fret if a parent was late home in case something had happened to them, but couldn't talk about it. It seemed silly, and in the daytime it didn't seem to matter so much.

My husband says that animals are happy in the moment because they don't have a concept of mortality. They just 'live' each day. It's a lesson worth learning within reason, but not easy.

So, let's get back to fear.

Heavens, it comes and comes; the fear of ageing, of trying something new. I've no comment on ageing. I've done the pinch test too, and didn't like the result, but the fear of trying something new? Think of it as a challenge. What is the worst that can happen?

There's the fear of being alone, of making an idiot of oneself.

There's the fear of saying no, or of being hurt.

Sometimes we refuse to love, just in case. What a gift we are rejecting. Loving and being loved is never wasted. Needing and being needed is a great gift.

Even if love does hurt, what good times there'll have been. What lessons we've learned. We're back to the concept that roads are for travelling along, not just for arriving.

Fear. The list goes on and on.

We mustn't let fear dominate, or hold us back, or take the colour from our lives.

We must keep reminding ourselves that we are living in the present, with an eye to the future. We mustn't ignore the 'now'.

We must savour it and make it count. We mustn't live a life unfulfilled. We must find courage. We must find peace in ourselves.

Let's give fear merely the space it warrants. It can keep us safe, but it shouldn't paralyse us.

My coping mechanism when a situation arises in today's world is to create a Plan A and a Plan B. Then I try to forget about it. This is a tip I learned from planning novels - two possible roads.

Enough chatting. Write about being lost. Or if you were never lost, imagine how it must have felt. Or ask someone who was, even if it was only for a moment, a heart-stopping moment.

Day 2

Think back to your first memorable birthday party.

The boys in our gang never asked the girls to their parties, but the girls had to ask the boys.

When I was eight I made a stand and hid the boys' invitations under the sofa cushions instead of delivering them. Their mothers complained. Mine was furious with me. Fresh invitations were issued.

I spent the party under the table, sulking, powerless. But was I? I had expressed myself, made my protest.

On the occasion of the children's party, it's clear that there were other agendas at work, the politics of a community.

I'll remember it now, however, from a child's point of view. Think how powerful it would be if you could successfully mix the two together. You might like to try and pick out these layered scenes in either a book or drama, or paintings, in other words, the theme behind the image.

The cloth hung down. It was dark...

Whilst thinking back to your memorable day, remember also the run up, the sequence of events, the event itself and the aftermath. Go on, back in time. Why was it memorable? Why? How?

You can probably see how this thought process, this questioning is enabling you to steer your thoughts into a logical sequence of events. This is helpful when you come to pursue your chosen creative medium, for all creativity eventually needs organisation and shape.

Day 3

Would you like to be a belly dancer? Go on, imagine what it would be like and write about it. How do you move, where do you look? Where would you most like to perform? Perhaps in a sheik's tent way back when?

Empathise.

Be in the body of the dancer, be her. Stand up, hear the music, feel the chiffon moving around her legs, the heat of the sun on the tent. If you decide belly dancing isn't for you, why not?

By the way, how do they stick that jewel in their navel? With chewing gum, as I did once? No, that story is for another day.
If you're a man, perhaps you'd rather think in terms of a male flamenco dancer? Think of high

heels - ouch - that tight waistcoat, the castanets, the clapping of the crowd. Empathise, be him.

Day 4

Put on gloves. Find a piece of cloth, a piece of wood, and something else from the garden or park. Place them on a tray. Remove the gloves. Shut your eyes and finger them. What are they like? Not what are they, but what are they like? Remember all the senses.

Is there something ribbed like a chocolate flake? (Don't you just love flakes? Can't you taste them, here and now?) Is there something smooth? Smooth, like? Can you come up with some wild and wonderful associations?

Let your mind play, and be that child again, the one who's always picking things up to feed the senses, to discover the touch, the sight, the sound, to understand this world, and their place in it.

Day 5

Recapture a cinema trip as a child. Did you go to Saturday morning cinema? Perhaps you're too young to have experienced that wonderful couple of hours? Anyway, when you went to whatever cinema, did you always drip choc ice down you? Did you have to sit at the back to avoid feeling sick? I can remember, one day… No, let's not go into that.

Day 6

Time out.

OK, so what are you doing today? Whatever it is, have fun.

Maybe by now if you're interested in pursuing the writing path, you've found a local writing group? Or is it to be painting? Or maybe you're reaching out, communicating more fully with those you meet? Or you probably don't know, and are just enjoying the journey.

If you have joined a creative group, remember that like-minded friends are important. They reassure you, reinforce your efforts.

But work to your own expectations, not the expectations of others.

I'll come to the mechanics of finding the right group on pages 58 and 71.

Personal notes

Creating a helpful environment

I know I said I wasn't going to go on about the daily pages, and the 'time alone' but... but...

I hope you're keeping it up. As my recompense for the nag, let's make your writing life more comfortable and create a helpful environment

Friends:

It might be an idea to step back a little and judge who are your supporters. By this I mean those who encourage and nurture your efforts to do this work. Spend more time with them.

'Here she goes again. What does she mean?'

It's good to be aware of the difference between those who nourish and those who control.

Those who nourish, cheer you forward and delight in your progress.

Those who control, make themselves essential to your efforts. They make you feel that without their support you won't succeed. They caution against flying too soon.

You don't need that control.

Now, I'm not saying drop them as friends, I'm just saying be aware of their existence. Not just for your development as a creative being, but in your life.

Conserve your energy. It's sad to squander it on those who ask too much of your time. Hey, can you take me to..? Or on those who obsessively talk of their problems. It's so often the same old problem, one from which they can't bear to part.

As long as you're there, you're promoting their dependence on you, and the problem. You're colluding in their stalled recovery.

I am not suggesting you walk away, just do enough, and no more.

Include yourself in your life. That's the word. Include. Not become totally self-obsessed. Just include yourself. You owe all those years in your mind that much. You owe the child that was you.

Be aware, too, that you can write anywhere, anytime. In planes, trains or automobiles. Just keep a notebook with you.

Personal notes

Third set of exercises

Day 1

List those who try to control you. List those who help and nourish. Write about the first person to nourish you. You can't remember? Imagine. You don't understand about control? Look it up in the library. The librarian will help you locate the right books, or why not try the Net? Understand the subtleness of some control, and the blatant nature of others.

Day 2

Go in your mind to your favourite beach. Shut your eyes. Sit on the sand, or is it shingle? Open your eyes, and look at the sea, listen to it. Is it the middle of the day? Can you feel the heat? Are there clouds? Are the waves pounding, or sweeping?

Just sit there, let the sand or shingle trickle through your fingers. You're alone. Just be there, on the beach. What else can you see, hear, touch, smell, taste? What is happening around you, above you? You haven't a favourite beach? Then be there, at your favourite spot, wherever it is. Write it up.

Day 3

You're still there on the beach, or whatever you choose as your favourite spot. You're sitting in the same place at the same time. Look to your right. There's a small child walking towards you. The child is getting closer. It's you, when you were young. What do you look like? Are you smiling, laughing, or thinking?

The child sits next to you. What does the child say to you about the things that worry him or her? The things the child has done and ought not to have done, the fears that won't go away? What do you say to comfort that child?

The child is you before experience shaped you. Comfort and reassure the child. What does the child say about where you are now? In his or her turn, the child will understand and forgive you those things that you cannot forgive yourself.

The two of you will celebrate the good times in your past. The child might remind you of dreams you once dreamt. Who knows? Only you know. What is the child that was you, saying? What do you say to the child, about the dreams you now have, and the fears?

Are you living the life the child wanted you to live? If not, can you accommodate a change? Is there any need? Is the present path capable of development? Write it up.

Day 4

You're on the beach, same time, same place, with the child sitting to your right. You look to the left. There is an older person walking towards you. It's you, the future you. What do you look like? Are you smiling? You'll be wiser.

The older you sits down to your left.

What do you talk about? What sort of a fist does the older person think you're making? Is the older you pleased with the direction in which you're taking her/him?

Spend time with the older you, talk, listen. It might just be a meeting of minds, not voices.

Discuss your dreams, your hopes and fears. What does the future you say? Are you living a life that's on the right road for the future you?

The sun is going down now. It's cooler.

The child on your right rises and walks away, and so too, does the older you.

Write up your conversation with your older self.

Day 5

Think of someone you might be controlling. Think of someone you are nurturing. Why are you doing these things? Or write about someone you admire. You'll find that they are not without flaws, but those flaws don't detract.

Remember not to strive for perfection
in yourself.
Instead, be as kind as you would be to someone else.

Or write about someone you absolutely do not admire. Why?

Think of reasons why they are as they are. Try to put yourself in their place and really understand them. Are they redeemable? If so, how? I'm encouraging you to empathise, which is essential for creativity. You might like to steal time for all the above alternatives.

Day 6

Time out. Will you go to a museum, the sea, a tea dance? Or maybe you'll shop? Perhaps you'll watch a film at the cinema?

Whatever you do, wherever you go, whoever you are with - be aware, soak up the experience, but find time to daydream as well.

Personal notes

Fourth set of exercises

It's that time again. Another six days of discovery. There's a belief that endeavour mustn't be enjoyed. Why? There's a belief that it's more worthy if it's drudgery. Phooey.

Enjoy your creativity. Savour it. You don't need to make it into toil for it to be acceptable to you or others.

Day 1

Look out of your window. What can you see? Write about it for 30 minutes. As an example, picture a man with a limp walking along. How did he get the limp? Does it bother him?

Oh, I know you can't look into him as though he is a crystal ball. But what do you think? What do you imagine?

How has it affected his present, his future? In other words, how has his past affected his present and future?

How has it made him who he is? If someone hurt him, has that someone carried guilt?

Be in him, be of him and everyone concerned. Let your Dreamweaver provide answers.

You are probably finding it easier now to let go, to loosen up enough to melt into, and be aware of other situations, to ask questions.

Your imagination is becoming increasingly used to being stirred. You're writing it awake, writing your creative self into existence, thinking laterally, conjuring up scenarios, personalities, dreams.

Day 2

List three things you like doing. Describe them. Describe the joy they make you feel. Allow yourself that joyousness. There's nothing that gives you joy? When was there something?

Day 3

List three things that you dislike doing. Describe them. Describe how they make you feel. Let it rip. See what you say.

Day 4

Write on why monks become monks, or nuns become nuns. You don't know? Then think about it, long and hard. Write about it, as though you are the monk, or nun. You're an atheist? What has that got to do with it?

Write about it. Get into that person.

Consider the problems they might have had to overcome to take that step, and the future they envisaged should they not be able to take the step. Did they turn away from the challenge to begin with, and then accept it? Surely there was some hesitation?

Surely there was a momentary rejection of the challenge, a turning away from the opportunity that would take them from their normal world onto the path leading to another?

What would be their considerations? What would their future be, had they stayed in their normal world? What would their future be once they accepted the opportunity? Would either path be free of doubts and difficulties? Would there be obstacles to be overcome?

There's a lot to think about here. So I hope you're reading all the exercises in the morning, and letting the Dreamweaver help you throughout the day.

If you want to know more, or can't get to grips with the subject at all, put it on hold. When you've time, drop into your library and ask the librarian. Or search the Net. Ask a monk, or a nun. Get used to reaching out, to asking questions, but with tact and gentleness. Know when to stop.

Day 5

Revisit a moment of success. What was it? Describe how it felt at the time. Describe how it feels to remember it.

Day 6

It's playtime.

Personal notes

More tips on creating a helpful environment

I'm taking for granted that you're writing your daily pages. I'm taking it for granted that you're putting pen to paper, even when it's too much trouble, even when you've nothing to say. Even when inspiration has galloped off across the horizon yelling, '*Writing? You cannot be serious.*'

I'm taking it for granted that you're having your time alone each day, and that you're writing your statements, if that appeals to you.

I'm taking it for granted that time out is never missed, and you're becoming familiar with being kind to yourself.

Perhaps, though, you're feeling a bit raw again? A bit as though your nerve endings are exposed? This will pass. Perhaps it hasn't happened at all? That's fine. It's all fine.

Perhaps you're feeling solitary? Have you refined your creative direction? If so, have you a creative friend? Even if you have, take a few steps to finding the workshop or class to suit you.

No information in the library? What about the local arts centre? Or try the local adult education centre. Please ensure that if there is a leader in the group, they're experienced, and that the tone of the group suits you. In other words, ask if you can sit in on one session and test the water.

Don't be shy of asking for what you want. As long as the approach is made tactfully everyone knows where they stand.

If you're still drawing a blank, try starting a workshop, or group of your own by writing to the local paper. They may well run a piece on the need for one. Or why not suggest that one of the organisations I've mentioned set one up. Or just put a notice in the local library, or arts centre.

But once with your new friends, don't let anyone hurry you through the 'release, reclaim, reveal' process. Don't doubt yourself or your progress when someone asks, *'It's all very well, but where is this leading? For what market are you writing, playing, painting?'*

You're laying the foundations from which you will spring. These foundations are essential. Don't rush. If it's beyond the comprehension of the group, then it might not be the right one for you. If you start a workshop, make this clear from beginning. If you've joined an established group, one that is intractable on this point, you may have to leave. That's OK, we've already discussed starting your own.

Learn to say no, it won't lead to being cast into outer darkness.

I expect a lot of you haven't yet found your creative avenue. That's fine. There's probably a general group or, if not, start one. There you'll be, a group of like minded explorers, all enthusing one another, all extending one another's creativity.

This group might be interested in attending a few lectures on local history. Perhaps you should try a theatre trip, or a concert? Let yourself receive other people's creativity and interests. Let yourself absorb, appreciate, and ask yourself why you enjoyed it. What did it give you? If you didn't enjoy it, I wonder why?

Try sitting in on the local Amateur Dramatic Society. Follow the process from the start. See how they choose a play, then cast it, direct it. It is another form of creativity at work, one that takes place around the 'day job'.

Acting involves people having to put themselves into the souls of their characters. Isn't this what you, as a writer or artist will try to do?

Don't potters have to become in tune with the clay as well as the subject?

Don't communicators have to understand those they talk and listen to?

Perhaps you'll find that play writing becomes a love of yours. Perhaps you'll land a part and be an actor, perhaps you will act, write, sing, <u>and</u> dance. Perhaps you'll see every play you can. Who knows? That's what so exciting.

Or you'll discover you're a writer. If so, there are residential courses like Arvon and Ty Newydd, and numerous painting, pottery, drama courses all over the country and abroad, and somewhere there's a circus school. There has to be. Use the Net to track them down, and yet again your local library.

Personal notes

Fifth set of exercises

Day 1

When did you last test yourself physically? When did you last ride a bike, a horse, a motorbike? Do you miss it? Did you like it, hate it, or both? If you loved it, perhaps you should try it again? How did it make you feel physically and psychologically whilst you were doing it, before you did it, after you did it? Write about it.

Day 2

Sit at your desk. Reach out and touch those things that are within reach, including yourself. Steady now, perhaps not the person sitting next to you.

Be aware of how everything feels. Be bold in your descriptions. How about a simile or a metaphor? Her skin is as smooth as silk - simile. Her skin is silk - metaphor. But don't worry about the terms unless you're really curious. If you are, find out. There's the library, the Net.

If you're heading towards writing, and serious reading, not to mention improved communication skills, then the terms might be useful for you to know. But it's enough, for now, to concentrate on awakening creativity. So just write.

Day 3

Sit at a table. Pick up a glass of water. Drink. Be aware of every action, every sequence of events. Be aware of the weight of the glass, the feel of it against your hand, against your lips and tongue. Does the glass touch your teeth? How do you swallow? Write it all down. Write for 30 minutes, or longer if you wish. But restrict yourself to this pin-hole scenario, this drinking event.

Day 4

Place a plate on the table. Put a fork on the plate. The fork has told the plate, ever since the plate has been able to listen, that the plate's ambition to spin on the top of a pole, beautifully and with elegance and in its own inimitable way, is irresponsible.

It's not what any sensible plate would do, the fork has always insisted, and it's just an attention seeking ploy. The fork is emphatic that the plate's attitude is selfish, and what's more, that the failure risk is high. He'd be bound to wobble, and fall, and then it would be noisy and messy as he broke into pieces. What's more, the plate would make a fool of himself and let the table down, and then the fork would have to find another plate to take his place.

The fork said that a plate's position in life was to be a plate, something useful, something that earned merit and didn't raise eyebrows. The fork said that a plate wasn't capable of such a feat, when it was such a round, flat thing.

The fork said it so often to the plate that deep within its core, the plate came to believe that it had no creative ability. Or, if it had, that it had no right to use it.

One day, a circus performer knocked on the door and approached the plate. He came with glue that would repair the plate should he fall. He had a plentiful supply of sawdust to lay beneath the pole. He has other plates that are longing to welcome him to the show and who made mistakes before they got the hang of it. They still make mistakes, but so what? Doesn't everyone? The circus performer tells the plate all of this.

The plate has a chance to take that step out of his ordinary world, if he has the courage. The plate realises at last that there is a moment of opportunity in everyone's life that opens the door to the future.

What does the plate say to the fork? What does the fork say to the plate? What do both say to the circus performer? I expect the plate will turn away from the opportunity. Most of us do, to start with. We don't want to leave the comfort zone. Can the circus performer change the plate's mind? What might the circus performer say? What about the fork? Would the fork say something unforgivable, something that triggered an acceptance of the opportunity by the plate?

Tough, isn't it? Go on, have a try at a conversation.

Has anyone consistently turned you away from your creativity, or discouraged your sense of self-esteem? Can you see how easy it is to awaken the Dreamweaver, and accept your own unique creativity, and with it a burgeoning self-esteem?

Can you accept this without any feeling of guilt, or shame? Can you accept it with joy and enthusiasm, and with a sense that it is your right, just as it is the right of everyone else?

Day 5

Look at these words. After. Over.

What do they mean to you? Think. Let them work on your own life experience.

What does the word 'After' mean to me?

How about? After I rode around Israel for charity, my life could never the same again. Why? I think it was because… I'll stop there, but now it's your turn. After. Over.

An extra today. Think, just think, about the facets of your past that most inform your present. Mine are events that have shaken my security, it's this part of myself that has had to be rebalanced.

The by-product of exploring and releasing creativity is that it allows you to spill out the angst, then re-arrange it, until you arrive at a deeper understanding and tolerance through your work.

The author Ernest Hemingway always insisted that writers should not flinch from these deep areas.

But again I say that if there are really difficult areas of your life that you choose not to visit, then make that decision.

Day 6

It's time out. Enjoy yourself.

Personal notes

A recap of the journey so far

The foundations of the rest of your life are taking shape. You've summoned your weaver of dreams. You've been creative and courageous.

Don't let the past reclaim these dreams. Hug them to you. Add new ones.

I hope that by now you're looking up at the clouds and imagining worlds within them.

I hope that you're saying, *'I can do this. I am doing this. Look at how much I've achieved. Look at all these words, these memories. I can touch that poppy. I can describe it. I can remember how it felt. If I can't remember, I can imagine.'*

I hope you can remember the heart-pumping terror/pleasure of the chase, the breath caught in your chest, the half laugh of fear. I hope you're not saying, *'People will mock. I'm wasting my time. This isn't earning me money, so how can I justify it?'*

I hope that you've written your statements, if the concept appealed to you, and found them helpful.

I hope that you have started to rebalance the negative aspects of your past using your writing, and your imagination. You'll find you'll use your experiences in your subsequent work. You'll shape them, borrow them to underpin an idea, to add a believable detail. Honour your past. It's who you are. It'll make you wise.

Personal notes

Sixth set of exercises

Day 1

Look at these words. Seek. Fall. Climb. What do they make you think about in your own life? Write about it.

Day 2

Close your eyes. Drop your shoulders. Relax. Let your thoughts run like a stream through the weeks or months of the course.

Pick one incident that has been important to you as we have progressed, and write about it. Write about what it meant to you, and of the response and reactions of others.

Day 3

Close your eyes. Drop your shoulders. Relax. Let your thoughts run like a stream through and around the last 10 years or so. Don't struggle to remember. You'll find that some events come to mind. Pick one, and write about it.

Consider what it meant to you, your feelings, the response and reactions of others. Can you put yourself in their place and consider the situation from their position?

Day 4

Close your eyes. Drop your shoulders. Relax. Let your thoughts run like a stream through the last twenty years, as though they are stepping-stones.

Don't struggle to remember. You will find that some events come to mind.

Pick one and write about it.

Consider what it meant to you, your feelings, the response and reactions of others.

Can you put yourself in their place? Can you see, feel, hear, taste and smell the event again?

Can you see, feel, hear, taste and smell it from someone else's point of view?

Day 5

Yes, you're nearly there.

Think of an opportunity you've missed, or rejected, a tiny opportunity, a huge opportunity.

Write about how your life might have been, had you taken up that chance to step away from your ordinary world.

Think of events that led up to this opportunity. The future considerations you mulled, the stages of your rejection.

Day 6

Time out.

It's up to you, but I think a huge celebration is in order.

You've worked hard and are well along the road we've taken together. It wasn't so difficult, was it?

You've taken so many steps; some tentative, some strong. Some have developed into strides.

You've this great swirling imagination, this acknowledgement of your past, this great appreciation of the world around you.

You've foundations on which to build the rest of your life. I wonder what you'll do, which roads you'll explore?

It's so exciting.

You've created time in your life for you. Don't let it fade away, back into the blur of every day life.

Keep the time, cherish it, use it to pursue your given path. Or use it to continue seeking. Or just use it, in any way you wish.

I hope that when you think of the older person who came to sit beside you on the beach, you feel he or she will approve of your present journey. For it's the route by which you will reach him or her.

Remember, above all, that you've the right to this time, these thoughts, this endeavour.

Remember to revisit any of these exercises in the future. They're your friends, they will remove blocks, and re-introduce you to the child within.

But hang on a moment, you're not quite finished yet. I have a bonus exercise, so read on.

Was that a groan I heard?

Remember, you are in control. You don't have to do it. You don't even have to look at it. But for those who want to, read on.

Personal notes

One final exercise

I'm now going to offer you an exercise that I do regularly. I find it refreshes and revitalises my creativity.

The word 'meditation' often conjures up images of caftans and beads but we all meditate, whether we realise it or not.

We've been a party to meditation when we've reached back into our past, when we've allowed the stream of consciousness to flow, when we've lost ourselves in the beauty of the sunset, the chords of stunning music, the heat of the sun on our faces. These are things we've experienced all through our lives.

I want you to pause and consider the phrase, 'Lost ourselves'. The concept is crucial.

The exercises we have been doing, whilst digging and delving into our lives have also helped us concentrate on things other than ourselves.

This concentration has trained us to be less self conscious, to reach out, to explore without embarrassment. In the process, we've not only found ourselves, but managed also to forget about ourselves.

This final exercise will reinforce this forgetting, and, at the same time, recharge our batteries.

Please do not feel you have to join in. It's perfectly fine to close the book and nip out for a coffee or a pint, but for those with a fleeting interest - join me. It is a good idea to record this and play it to yourself, once you have read it through. Or make up your own.

If you're sitting comfortably, let us begin.

Find a comfortable chair. Remove your shoes, place your feet square on the floor, and your hands palm up on your lap.

Breathe in through your nose, feel your chest and abdomen expand, then release your breath through your mouth, pulling in your stomach to expel the air from your lungs.

Do this three times, with your eyes shut. Let your shoulders drop and imagine that you are walking towards a wood on a hot summer's day.

Ahead of you is a gate, a green gate. The paint is peeling. It's a much used gate, one that leads to the woods and, after that, over a bridge to the beach. You love it here. You open the gate. It's warm to the touch. You walk through, then close it.

You walk along an uneven path. Beneath your shoes you can feel the stones, and a root of a tree. On either side, are flowers and trees, the odd trunk, mossy with ivy.

Above you, the sun is streaming through the branches. The leaves are rustling. You can see flowers: celandines, foxgloves, honeysuckle. You can hear the bees, the leaves.

You walk slowly, watching, listening, breathing in the scent of the woods.

Thoughts come into your head, and float away again as you focus on the foxgloves, pink ones, cream ones.

You see the bees. You hear them.

You stop and look whenever you want. It's warm, so warm. Way in the distance is the drone of a plane, the distant, distant drone.

On you walk, on and on and soon you can hear the stream, flowing gently.

You can see the bridge. It's lichen-covered.

Now you're stepping from the shade of the last tree into the bright sunshine and onto the bridge.

You stop in the middle. You touch the lichen. It's rough.

You look at the clear water, flowing so gently. You look, and look, and then you walk over the bridge. Ahead of you is a meadow, sweet with grasses, a meadow that moves as though it's a tranquil sea.

You take the path that runs to the left, along the bank of the stream. There's a dragonfly hovering in the reeds. The water is flowing, nudging the bank, nudging the stepping-stones.

Stop and look for a moment, hear the water.

Now, walk out onto the biggest stepping-stone. Listen to the water lapping the stone. It's staining the stone a darker colour. Stay as long as you like.

Return to the bank and walk on to the crest of a rise. The sky is blue.

The sea, too, spread out before you.

Can you smell it?

Can you hear the gulls, hear the surf on the shingle?

The stream runs between the high shingle bank out to sea. You walk on the shingle.

Hear it beneath your shoes. Feel it shifting as you walk. You make your way to a gentle rise and sit. Look at the sea, look at the sun on the swell. Feel the heat of the sun on your head, on your hands. It's not too hot. It's just right. There's a faint breeze.

When you're ready, look to your right.

Approaching is the child you once were.

The child is smiling at you, and comes to sit beside you, and together you watch the waves gently move in and out over the shingle.

There's no need for words. You know all there is to know about one another. There's only acceptance. But words can be spoken, if that's what you both want.

When you're ready, you both look to the left. Here is you, the future you, approaching.

The future you sits on your left, touches your shoulder, and smiles at you both.

All three of you sit and look and listen, and feel the sun.

There may be more words, there may not. The future and past you is glad you are being kind, and taking a moment of peace.

The future and past you is glad, because you hold his or her soul in the palm of your hand.

It's your actions that determine your future self's existence. Your younger self is glad that you're taking her/him with you into realms once hoped for.

You sit for as long as you like.

When it is time to return, you rise, all three of you.

Your younger self smiles with approval and encouragement and leaves, walking steadily away to the right.

Your future self smiles with approval, encouragement, and hope, and leaves, walking steadily to the left.

For a moment, you stand and feel the sea breeze, the sun. You watch the sea, you thank it for its beauty.

Now you walk back over the rise, along the bank of the stream.

The dragonfly is still there hovering amongst the reeds. The scent of the meadow grass reaches you, heightened by the heat of the sun, a seagull calls.

You reach the bridge, and slowly you cross into the cool of the wood.

You amble along the path, feeling the stones and the root beneath your shoes.

You see the foxgloves, the honeysuckle, the celandine, the bees. You hear the leaves rustling.

On you walk, and now you see the gate, which is lit by the sun. You reach it, touch it. It is warm.

You open it, pass through and close it behind you.

You're walking back up the path. As you walk, you breathe in deeply through your nose.

You feel your chest and abdomen expand.

You breathe out through your mouth, pulling in you stomach.

You breathe in again, and slowly your eyes open.

You expel the breath.

You breathe in once more, and expel it once more.

You stretch. You roll your shoulders. You're back.

Wait for a moment. Take all the time you need.

When you're ready, rise. Step on that roundabout called life, again.

Remember that the gate is always there for you. You just have to open it and step into the sanctuary of the wood for the calm to descend and for your energy to be restored.

Conclusion

It's now time for our paths to diverge. You'll go your way, and I'll go mine. It's been fun to be with you, explore with you and if you want to talk to me further, use my website. The address is at the end of this handbook.

You've endured to the end. You've created time in your life, which is never easy. You've put aside your ego, and explored what have, at times, been painful memories.

You've helped other, and better times to emerge.

I hope you've made other creative friends, and in particular, made a friend of yourself.

I hope you see life differently, more clearly, and in more depth.

I hope your own life has more substance, more understanding and tolerance of others, and yourself.

I hope that you will continue with your daily pages.

I hope it has been the start of an enduring journey that will bring opportunities and challenges, some of which you will accept.

I hope you find time to daydream, to just be, and allow inspiration to enter.

Releasing your creativity? Reclaiming your unique voice? Revealing the communicator within?

I can hear you saying, *'I know what she means, and I'm on the way. I have a unique voice, and I know exactly what a Dreamweaver is.*'

Most of all, I wish you well. I wish you the enjoyment of creativity, of conversation, of burgeoning self-esteem, and a life fulfilled.